TRUSTING
GOD
THROUGH THE
STORMS

Putting Faith into Action Amidst Trials and Adversity.

Anastasie Charles George

ISBN 978-1-64569-328-4 (paperback)
ISBN 978-1-64569-329-1 (digital)

Christian Faith Publishing, Inc.
832 Park Avenue
Meadville, PA 16335
www.christianfaithpublishing.com

Printed in the United States of America

Biography of Anastasie Charles George
Single Mother of Eight Overcoming Life Crises
Empowerment to Life's Success

Acknowledgments

First and foremost, I would like to give honor to my Lord and Savior Jesus Christ for granting me the inner strength and courage to overcome the many struggles, crises, and challenges during marriage, divorce, raising eight children as a single parent while attending higher and post education and being employed both full and part-time.

My inner strength could have only been accomplished by building a personal relationship with the almighty. It's comforting to know that even while going through my life circumstances, the Lord allowed me to achieve my goals, dreams, aspiration, and to overcome all the impossibilities of my life. What I realized throughout my personal journey is that I needed to totally depend upon the Lord knowing he has the power to restore all things. For we can never know the reality of God's purpose in our lives.

I thank my deceased aunt Philemon Edwards for her parental guidance, her positive influence in establishing a sound foundation in my life. Most of all, for the moral values instilled in me which have transformed my personality and identity.

Special gratitude to my eight children for being so patient and understanding during my journey while being absent from their presence most of the time. Because of my responsibility to provide for the family, I was also employed both full and part-time and attended college. It was not easy, but we supported each other believing that we were not defined by our trials and failures but becoming an overcomer. My children Johan, Pat, Rod, Patrick, Rick, Maria, Elrick, and Vernita have been truly a blessing in my life. Their love and support strengthened me during my journey.

To my best friend Peter who supported me and took time out his busy schedule to provide me with transportation to and from my internship while accomplishing my master's degree. I must say, it was truly a blessing for having these people in my life during this transition. I am very much appreciative for the support I received from everyone during my academic success.

My African American director whom I love dearly gave her unselfish passion without prejudice in acknowledging my potential throughout my career, giving me the opportunity to bridge into my target professional career. She was one of the best supervisors and director. She treated her employees with no prejudice and was often challenged by many of her subordinates.

Many of my challenges, critical forces, and crises could not have been overcome without the help of these wonderful people. I am happy to say that as an overcomer, I am no longer defined by my trials and failures. Having developed a strong faith, personal relationship, and a spiritual fulfillment with him, God gave me the strength to embrace the tough times and the unchangeable moments to move to the changeable.

Dedicated all to God who has pursued me persistently, loved me relentlessly and continues to teach me how to know him more and more through my trusting God through the storms.

Battling Survival Throughout The Storm

My name is Anastasie George. I was born in the Caribbean West Indies. Birth parents are Mary and Johnnie Charles. Johnnie is now deceased. I have nine brothers and six sisters. At the age of fourteen months, I was forced to live with my aunt, my father's sister, because of many life challenges, hardship, and other life circumstances. Unfortunately, as I grew into my teen years, I was sent to live with my dad in the Virgin Island. However, I later got married at age twenty-one and gave birth to six more children. By age thirty, I became the mother of eight wonderful children. During and after my marriage, I went through many life challenges, abuse, and economic hardship. Later, I relocated to the states to join my ex-husband where I gave birth to my eighth child. During that process, my life became a total disaster, but by the grace of God, I embraced the tough times and the unchangeable, trusting God even when I had no understanding of my life transformation. My only desire was to find a new purpose and destination for my life.

Professional Skills And Experience

- Graduate school of social work.
- LMSW group work, case work, community organizer,
- Provided therapeutic services to individuals and families of all diversities.
- Completed intake assessments, programs eligibility, counseled families and individuals.
- Made recommendations regarding <u>treatment</u> plans

- Administered Myers-Briggs assessment to identify occupational strength and weaknesses
- Created, developed, and designed cover letters and resumes for individuals
- As a Global Career Development Facilitator (GCDF), conducted and customized several job search and vocational exploration workshops
- Provided intensive case management services to customers
- Committed to helping families and assisted them reach a place of stability and wellness led to progress that helped clients resolve their involvement with the Department of Children Services.

Impactful Career Development And Certifications

- Diversity training
- Transforming The Way We Work
- Enhanced ReEmployment Service
- GCDF Empolyability Skills
- GCDF Helping skills
- Ethics and Case Notes
- Program Planning & Public Relations
- Technology in Career Development
- Working with Diverse Population
- Violence Prevention
- Role of LMI in Career Planning
- How to be Successful with the Hard to Employ
- Radar Approach to Job Retention
- Substance Abuse Training
- Conducting Effective Meetings
- Ethical Issues in the Workplace
- Public Relations for Office Support Staff

My Dark Moments and Challenges

Throughout my life, I was faced with various challenges and oppositions. I was not exempt from facing racism, homelessness, discrimination, divorce, abuse besides having to raise eight children on my own. At age thirty, I became a single mother of eight and was left with the entire burden of parenting. It seemed as though as one chapter of my life closed, another one was enfolding. By the grace of God, every door was unlocked to a brighter future. He freed me from my past, giving me freedom and success. I realized by totally depending upon God, everything finally will fall into place. Embracing faith and the courage to move forward was my greatest strength in recognizing my own weaknesses, allowing God to lead and to take total control. I utilized strategies that allowed me to cope on a daily basis.

As far back as my memories go, I remembered talking to God every minute, even while walking on the road. There were times I was approached by many asking whether I was alright because my lips constantly moved praying. I was too fearful to try talking to people who may have not being able to help situations, nor understand the painful moments of life challenges.

I finally developed personal strategies leading to a road map in maintaining balance in each area of my life.

Personal Strategies

- Faced the loss directly and did not isolate myself
- Discussed my feelings with friends, relatives whom I trusted
- Did not block out my feelings with negativities
- Allowed grief to progress naturally

- Did not suppress my feelings, accepted what could not be changed, and started a new beginning.
- Always find resolution during my painful moments as I learned to discharge my anguish and prepared to go on living.

Childhood Survival, a Miracle from God

Few months after I was born, I was faced with a situation between life and death. My family life circumstances changed within my family system where my dad decided to relocate for economic reasons, leaving the family behind. Although we had a great sense of community where each person looked out for each other, it was still a struggle financially. In fact, people were not as materialistic and individualist. If the neighbor knew you had no food, you definitely would not go to bed hungry. Emphasis was mostly placed on family traditional values, religious beliefs, moral values, and strong work ethics. The two most effective parenting styles were communication and discipline which have also been passed down to my immediate and extended family.

Unfortunately, a few months after my dad relocated, I went through a critical moment. The fact that I was in my infancy stage and things did not fall through as planned, the family suffered worst economic hardship. My biological mother was left with no alternative but to seek employment. I can truly say that single parenting is arguably and is one of the most difficult jobs in the universe whether brought on by death, divorce, or separation. This circumstance leaves a mom or dad to deal single-handed with traditional aspects of parenting and a whole lot more. The single parent must provide in all aspects, whether it's emotionally, financially maintaining the household as well as making sure the needs of the family is met and still find the energy at the end of the day to assure that the family is well secured. My mother said life circumstance was so hard that she actually saved the meals she received from work to feed her children.

At the time of her employment, she was left with no choice but to depend on her brother to care for me who had no formal experience or knowledge about parenting. My life was then in danger and at risk. I was neglected and left unattended most of the time by my inexperienced uncle who cared for me at the moment. After three months, I became very ill with little hope of survival. Had it not been for the Lord on my side, I probably would have been dead. The Lord truly had a special purpose for my life which indeed was a miracle.

One day unexpectedly, my aunt who is my father's sister decided to come to my rescue because she heard about the crises I was faced with. The fact is she lived about thirty miles away from my mother, never visited that city, and had little recollection of what my mother looks like. She was determined and desperate to intervene. Believe it or not, my aunt traveled miles in locating my biological mother. That morning, as my aunt walked over a bridge, she came in contact with a woman. She then introduced herself and started to inquire about a lady by the name Mary; she did realize she was communicating with my biological mother. As they continued to exchange information, they both realized they were not strangers as they thought. This was truly a miracle and not a coincident as what people was led to believe. I truly believe God has a plan and purpose for everyone regardless of our state and our circumstances. One must know God's immeasurable grace personally, knowing that he will always guide our path.

My aunt took me and traveled back to her city as she continued to seek interventions on my behalf. However, my situation got worst even though I was admitted to the hospital. It was now six months and had made very little improvement. My aunt stated, "Life did not look promising because most of the doctors said there was no chance of survival." She continued to pray, believing and hoping for a miracle. Yes, there is power in prayer. I believe prayer is the most powerful and effective weapon for those who trust God for answers and deliverance. My life is a living testimony. However, since I needed constant supervision and critical care, she asked the doctor to discharge me. My dear aunt never gave up. Indeed she consulted all and every herbal naturopathic as well as implementing her own natural remedies.

Finally, my health improved and was able to walk again. My cousin Georgina expressed several times how she assisted my aunt in caring for me throughout my illness, which is much appreciated. I do believe as children of God, we have the power over darkness and every stronghold that comes against us. For with God, all things are possible. I have no doubt about the fact that it was God who planted the seed into my aunt's heart. I will always be forever grateful for the love and sacrifices my aunt made in caring for me during those dark moments.

One may ask, "Well, how do you know all of this?" Let me share this with you. I remembered there was a day my aunt reprimanded me for being disobedient. I was so upset that I told her she was not my mother, I didn't have to listen to her and that she should never scold me again. She was so hurt that she cried for two days. The next day, my aunt sat me down and explained everything she went through to save my life. She also presented to me the clothes in which I was dressed as well as the shoebox I was placed in at the time she carried me back to her hometown. My life is truly a miracle.

My aunt was a loving, caring, devoted Catholic who had strong moral values. She loved everyone especially the community at large. She would do anything to save lives whether she knew you or not. She was just that type of person. What I admired most about my aunt was her great philosophy about promoting education. She made sure that I attended school every day and encouraged me to do my best. Even if I wanted to disappoint her, I could not. Although she could not read nor write, she strongly emphasized and encouraged me to obtain higher education. She always reminded me that education will always be the key to success and that I should strive very hard to obtain it to the highest level. I was forced to spend most of my time reading and attending private lessons after school five days a week. I felt like a prisoner because I had no time to socialize like most children, but I guess it paid off.

I am truly grateful for her instructions and parental guidance which allowed me to implement and obtain higher and post education. I am very much appreciative for my aunt's discipline and guidance from infancy to adulthood. This could never have happened without her parenting guidance. I will be ever so grateful for my loving, diseased aunt whom I miss so dearly. My only regret is that she did not leave to see my accomplishments in achieving post education, having obtained my LMSW (Licensed master Social Worker).

When my aunt died, part of me died also. I felt like my entire world collapsed because whenever there was a crisis in my life, I always consulted her, and I would be comforted. She was always concerned and wanted the best for me. In fact, she was devastated when she learned that I was separated /divorced at an early age, having to bear the burden of caring for eight children by myself. We, indeed, had a very strong bond between us.

My aunt became very ill and was not aware of her illness, because she kept it a secret from me for fear of causing stress upon my life. Because of my close relationship with God, it was revealed to me one day while sitting at my desk at work. My spirit was so troubled and overwhelmed, not understanding what was happening, later that day a strong feeling came over me that my aunt was very ill, so I immediately requested the time off and flew to visit her. Upon my arrival she was very surprised because I never notified her in advance. As soon as I entered the door, she embraced me and started weeping, by then we both wept bitterly as we tried to console ourselves. She then discloses her illness and requested her wishes regarding her death in case she dies after my return. I supported and cared for my aunt until the day she passed.

Ten minutes before my Aunt died she called me over the phone thanking me, for caring and providing her needs, stating God will bless me for all my deeds. Stating how she loves me and that god will truly bless and reward me. It never dawn to me at the moment that this would be her last breath. Too often times our shame and guilt paralyzes or imprison our minds which hinders our progress and freedom. We should always try to leave peacefully with all men, hold no grudges or resentment, because we never know when our last breath will be taken away from us.

Trusting God Even When I Did Not Understand

What a miracle to know that God's unmeasurable grace indeed saved me. He had a special calling and purpose for my life. Unfortunately, most children tend to suffer critical damages during family separation such as neglect, abuse, not having adequate food, shelter, etc. Children who are cared for by single parents seem to have suffered several crises and is more likely to suffer financial burdens and emotional problems.

Most homes are faced with difficult times or even coming to the worst times ever. During such crises, we tend to make the hardest decisions, even immediate decisions. Personally, I embraced a spiritual approach in facing and handling my personal and family crises with the faith and confidence in God's transcendence over time and the victory to overcome each trial. The fact is I truly believe if we walk with God and trust him, he will never leave us alone. The key to success and empowerment lies in faith, obedience, and endurance. The nature of critical episodes can be as varied as life circles itself, whether divorce, marital problems, homelessness, unemployment, illness, parenting, or financial dilemmas seriously affects the routine of our daily life.

My faith allowed me to regain strength and empowered me to overcome my failures, disappointments, and other forms of barriers. We are all God's divine creation and that we all are given a choice to realize we are free to choose our own master but choosing carefully. The power of choice is in our hands. We can either choose God as the maker of our soul journey depending upon his strength for guidance even when we cannot understand the purpose of our crises.

Much time, we often blame God or others for the pain and sufferings in our lives instead of seeing the situation as a test or stepping stone to our favor and victory. Too many times, we dismiss God and push love away when we have been wounded. For we have a tendency to make the worst choices when we are going through our worst times.

Once I began to let go of my past, forgave those who hurt me, God's blessings became effective into my life. This was the only true way of moving forward, believing and knowing victory and justice belongs to God. Who can stand before God? No one can, and no one will, for victory belongs to him. For in him I found true peace, happiness, and contentment.

I will always declare victory throughout my circumstances through the power of prayer. Remember, time waits for no man. Our excuses, indecisiveness, regrets, anger, and pride will not turn back time. So please, learn to let go of the past, and spend your time with the right purpose, deeds, and emotions. These characteristics demonstrates the depth of our spiritual growth. (a) We should always live a life that has undivided focus and devotion to the lord (b) write down specific goals to enrich our spiritual growth (c) Must be accountable to God.

Life Transformation: Finding a New Purpose

After graduating from high school, my aunt decided it was time for me to explore my career choices. Therefore, she decided to send me to meet my dad. Three months after my arrival, I was faced with numerous critical forces. My father's wife decided that I was not welcome for any absolute reasons and requested that I seek shelter elsewhere. I believe the fact that my dad was still legally married to my mother and that my dad was in this new relationship with having five children complicated everything. My father was placed in a very difficult situation but, finally, divorced my mother and married her. My biological mother is now 86 years old, very active, loves to travel.

My dad, whom I loved dearly, made arrangements for me to live with one of his friends which negatively impacted my life. At the time, I felt rejected, humiliated, and powerless while my faith in God was questioned, even though my only hope of survival was to trust God. This situation forced me into a relationship that I was never prepared for. Five months after the relationship, I got pregnant with my first child. I was nineteen years of age, very naïve, since I was raised very sheltered by my aunt. I had not been exposed to life experiences in terms of intimate relationships. I was so downcast and broken that I walk out of the relationship seven months into my pregnancy. I went to live with my biological mother where my child was finally born.

One year after the birth of my child, my biological mother decided that it was time for me to return to my child's father for fear of him neglecting and abandoning the child. I was totally unprepared to get back into this relationship, but because I was left with no other alternatives, I went back to meet the very same person I never wanted to live with since we argued most of the times, I finally separated myself and walked away.

It was very difficult to make any commitment to this relationship even though we are still very good friends. As humans, there are times that we are forced to stay into relationships that are toxic for various reasons, but we must commit our first love to the Lord, renew our minds, and establish closeness to him. A healthy relationship always requires a clear perspective of oneself. Anyone who stays in unhealthy relationships always suffers further repercussions. Please carefully consider the sequences that you could follow before making stupid mistakes because some of the mistakes may be repairable but can never be forgotten.

Going back to live with my baby's father was the worst thing ever. We argued most of the time especially at evening. Emotionally, I was not prepared to get back into this relationship a second time, and therefore, I suffered the consequences. However, my baby's father decided he was not going to have me cohabit because he wanted to have an intimate relationship. So one evening, he forced himself on me. The following day, I left his house and went to live with a cousin of mine whom I had just met a month prior to the incident. Two months later, I realized I was pregnant. I felt so hurt with the situation that I decided not to discuss it with anyone nor disclose the pregnancy to him.

The fact of the matter is I never spoke to him again nor had any contact with him for a long time. However, my daughter was now twenty-two years of age, and I decided to tell her who was her real father. Both of his two children and I do have a very good relationship because I totally commit my life into the hands of God, his love enables me to forgive and forget the past and extend the same love to others regardless of the situation. The fact is women tend to stay in abusive relationships for fear of the unknown; some probably are looking for affection and may not want to do without the partner once they find it, or they may feel comfortable with the relationship because there are children involved and have no other alternatives. Filled pleasured by a loving, generous, protective man may seem right, but once they become abusive, they should be left alone. No women should have to say in abusive relationships for the sake of children or sexual desires. For God is not an author of confusion but of peace. For the wisdom that is from above is first pure, then peaceable. If we have an unbelieving spouse who refuses to live peacefully and wants to depart let him go, for we are not under bondage. Just be cognitive of the fact that we are still committed to walk perfect before god and that there is always room for reconciliation during the marriage covenant.

These conditions cause much struggles and pains, and therefore, women should never enable their partner. As women, we are not bonded to live in such abusive relationships nor become a sex object but should be treated with respect and dignity. We should never allow our disappointments to take away our joy and hope. We can always reclaim our freedom in Christ, power, and restoration to happiness.

My life was totally dependent upon the Lord for relief and restoration, knowing that as long as his hands was upon me, I could never be defeated.

I am very encouraged by the book of Joshua chapter 1 verses 7 as I applied these words. "For the lord said, be not afraid, neither be thou dismayed for the lord thy God is with thee where so ever thou goes't."

Trusting God. Allows us to actively pursue happiness, knowing that happiness doesn't come from wealth, beauty, status, or anything external, but from within. We should never rely on others for happiness, because our life will always be endlessly disappointed. So accept responsibility for your own happiness as well as your self-worth.

Trusting God Even When
I Don't Understand

While living with my cousin, I came in contact with a young man who seems to be the dream and desire of every young woman. He was very charismatic, caring, and had a loving attitude. We were very much attracted to each other and, therefore, became friends for a while and, later, began dating. At the time I was pregnant with my second child, I disclosed the pregnancy to him and was willing to take full responsibility. He accepted my conditions and loved both me and the baby unconditionally.

The young man was a caring, loving individual who understood what I was going through at the moment; we were open and honest to each other in sharing almost everything. He refused for me to have an abortion even when I wanted to. I did not want to rest this burden upon him. He was very empathic and supportive during my pregnancy. He asked me not to abort the child and that he would take full responsibility which he did. Could you believe that even when I decided to have an abortion, he insisted that I should keep the baby? He treated the baby with no prejudice but love it as his own. As a matter of fact, he gave the baby his last name. Looking back, as I recalled, this is the best decision ever; my daughter is so loving and protective of me. As well as having a very good mother and daughter relationship.

We all have the free will to make choices in our daily lives. We live in a society that promotes pro-choice, while some people are for and some are against having an abortion. Personally, I decided not to have an abortion despite my circumstances which has truly been a blessing for the great relationship my daughter and I have developed.

In spite of how critical those crises may be in our lives, we should never doubt God's grace and his loving kindness, knowing that he is a god of restoration. No matter what happens in our lives, we have the power to rise up above it as long as we continue to speak life into our circumstances. Remember, the word of the Lord said, "Death and life is in the power of the tongue, those who love it shall eat the fruit thereof." So please speak life into your circumstances.

A year later, the young man asked me to marry him, which I did. The same night of our wedding, my third child was conceived. I must confess that this was the happiest moment of my life for the fact that I finally found someone who loved me as much as I loved him and had many things in common. People always told me they believe my marriage was made in heaven because of the relationship we shared.

Seventh year into our marriage, my husband began socializing with friends who did not have his best interest at heart. We started having problems. He became so insecure that I had to be careful who I talk too, otherwise, he would inflict me. By then, he had developed some bad habits and was also under the influence of alcohol which caused much conflicts throughout the marriage. The worst thing a person can do is not identify who their true friends are. These friends of his were divorced and also consumed alcohol. My husband never had a problem getting out of bed for work, but because of his decision to please his friends, he now was unable to keep a job for the lack of motivation. Our relationship and finances got so bad that he decided to move to Washington to live with his brother in order to seek employment, which was also unsuccessful.

Marriage is truly a covenant made between God and man. If we do not understand the agreement and covenant of marriage, we will never be able to protect it. Covenants cannot operate without the ongoing involvement of God. When the practical realities of God are dismissed from marriage, it becomes an invitation to the adversary to create havoc, pain, and destruction especially when children are involved.

My caring, loving husband and father of my children was now transformed into a total stranger. His drinking habits caused him to lose every job. The friends whom he socialized with had a negative influence upon his life. I was so disappointed with my marriage, realizing the reality was different from the life I dreamt. When I got married to my husband, neither of us were born-again Christians, but soon after, I accepted the Lord, but he never did. I accepted the Lord as my personal savior six years after I married my husband which he chose not to. I made many mistakes during my walk with God; yet, he never gave up on me. The Lord continued to shower me with his grace and mercies and also carried me throughout my life circumstances. What made matters even worse is that I was now married to someone who shared different beliefs. The same thing that happened to me can happen to anyone. There was no more compatibility between us. I strongly encourage marrying someone who has similar beliefs and is compatible so that you can grow spiritually together. Too many times people marry for the wrong reasons.

We had our shares of conflicts as life circumstances progressed things from bad to worst. My life was much stressed. I learned to cope with each situation through faith and prayer, hoping for a miracle for the sake of my children. I learned to forgive my husband daily by accepting God's grace as I delighted myself in the Lord.

I lived a very stressful life; by the time my sixth child was born, I became very ill and underwent surgery. During that time, my children were not able to care for themselves because they were only one year apart. The eldest was only seven. My children were cared for by church members with limited support from their father which I will always be grateful for. I must say he was a man who love and cared about his family before converting into this other person. There are certain memories and pains of my life which can never be forgotten even though I forgave my ex-husband.

While recuperating from my illness, my two-year-old son climbed up the chest medicine cabinet in the bathroom where he got hold of my prescription and eat the tablets; it was indeed a nightmare. By the time I discovered the incident, it was too late because the medication had already passed through his bloodstream. My son fell asleep about 6:00 p.m. and never woke up even that following day. That was when I realized something had to be definitely wrong.

I tried to wake him up, but he just would not respond, so I took him to the emergency room. I was told he had been overdosed with medication and that there was very little they could do because the medication had gone into his bloodstream. He had to be monitored on a daily basis, not knowing what the outcome would be like. This was the most frightening moment of my life because my son was badly affected. He could not walk nor talk, almost paralyzed. I spent sleepless nights weeping, not knowing what the outcome would be, whether my son would ever walk or talk again. Few months later, my son regained total consciousness and was able to take baby steps until he finally became mobilized. He is now a college graduate and is now employed as an educator. I thank the almighty for blessing me with such another miracle.

I believed God allowed me to go through these crises to transform me into becoming the person I am today. For when we trust him even when we do not understand why, he will see us through. The Lord stood by my side again and again even when I couldn't carry myself. He did not allow me to carry those burdens alone; for his words promised that he will never leave me nor forsake me. I trusted his counsel.

God's Calling on My Life

My first encounter with God was that evening when God spoke to me in a very loud voice. It's an experience I can never forget. As I recall clearly, that evening, I was contemplating to take away my life because the burdens of my heart became so intensified. I felt I had no reason to live. God spoke to me that moment. While weeping, I heard a loud voice which said, "Trust me, God, don't trace me." That was repeated three times. I got so fearful that I quickly went down on knees in prayer, asking the Lord for forgiveness.

Here came another great miracle. Four months after having surgery, I got pregnant with my seventh child. I almost got a nervous breakdown, but by the grace of God, I survived this storm. It was the conditioning of my mind along the strength of the Lord that enabled me to successfully overcome those challenges. I realized, in order for me to overcome those challenges, I must have a true perspective of who I am. A healthy relationship always requires a clear perspective of oneself. The question one should always ask is, "How can we build strong bonds with our spouse if we don't even know ourselves, whether, physically, psychologically, emotionally, and spiritually?"

Immediately following the birth of my seventh child, my husband finally relocated to Washington, D.C. to seek employment. At that time, our finances was so bad that the house which I lived with my seven children went into foreclosure.

My children were ages ten, eight, six, five, four, three, and one. Having no financial support or family system, life was truly a challenge. It was the most devastating moment of my life. Each day was a struggle just to provide the basics of life for my children. While experiencing these conditions, my only alternative was to trust God even more and to build my inner strength in the supernatural, God himself. My personal experience has allowed me to build a deeper and meaningful relationship with God, making him the most valuable person in my life.

The fact is every parent wants to give their children the best quality of life, which was not possible. This was when I really began to apply more faith in God, trusting every moment for a miracle. I have always been a firm believer of the word of God, praying, and fasting. Every moment of my life was spent believing God with his promises, knowing that one day, life will get better, and I will be an over-comer. *His words promised never to leave me nor forsake me.* And I believed it, even though there were times I doubted myself because of the various barriers I had to overcome such as lack of transportation, childcare, unemployment, housing, finance, etc. I continued to apply more faith in the Lord because I believe and trusted his words. My deep sense of spirituality allowed me to overcome my fears, develop high self-esteem, and take control in empowering my life situation as I became very proactive as I faced all my challenges.

Two years after my husband's departure, I gainfully found employment which gave me the opportunity to provide my children their needs and avoid the house going into foreclosure. I remembered like it was yesterday. When the loan officer approached me with the paperwork and saw that I had all these helpless children, he immediately decided to work something out to avoid me losing the house. He said to me that if I can come up with one payment by the following month, then he would stop the foreclosure. I struggled and suffered much economic hardship, but the Lord saw me through. It was indeed another miracle.

God worked miraculously throughout my life circumstances; my deep sense of spirituality and my faith in God, through much prayer and perseverance, gave me the strength and courage to go on. One Sunday evening as I attended church service, the pastor made a request and asked for a special love offering. I did not know who that special love offering was for, neither had I ever disclosed my life circumstances to him. That Sunday evening, I had only ten dollars and said, "Lord, you know this is all the money I have in my possession, but I trust you for a blessing" as I put five dollars into the love offering. At the end of the service, I received a call from the pastor stating that the love offering was for me because the Lord had laid it on his heart. I can truly say I am living testimony of experiencing the promises of God. What a miracle; I needed three hundred and fifty-three dollars to pay the mortgage to prevent the house going into foreclosure, and the love offering collected had exactly three hundred and fifty-five dollars. God works in mysterious ways even when we do not understand.

As a single parent, my key responsibility was to find means and ways to provide for my children. I needed healing and fulfillment to gain the strength needed to bring stability into my life. People may never understand and know the tears that I shed at night behind closed doors. Sometimes, instead of dealing with our challenges, we tend to run away from them which makes things even more complicated. For God said, "Seek ye first the kingdom of God and his rightness and all the things you need shall be added unto you."

Since marriage and family life was my alternative lifestyle, it was very difficult to amend to another lifestyle. I ensured continuity in transmitting my beliefs each day even though there were times I developed strong feelings of discouragement.

After my husband relocated to Washington, he practically abandoned the family. Two years later, I received a letter with a five-dollar bill. It might be hard to believe, but it came in timely and was much appreciated because that day, I was praying to God, asking to send me at least $5.00 which I needed to buy medication for my two-year old. I began to cry, and as my tears flowed, the children surrounded me and asked, "What happened, Mommy?" They were too young to understand the meaning behind those tears. Imagine, I needed $4.75 to buy the medication and received the $5.00 soon after pleading to God. I know there is power in prayer which I will never cease to pray. No matter what the circumstance may be, just believe, *for godliness with contentment is great gain*. As a single parent, I know what it's like to play both roles, taking full responsibilities, caring for eight children.

It has been scientifically proven that women have more neural connectors between their limbic brain and the prefrontal cortex than men. The prefrontal cortex is commonly called the thinking brain. It is the area of the brain that causes us to think critically about our lives, figure things out, follow through perseverance, control our impulses, learn from our experiences, express our emotions, and create empathy for those who are less fortunate.

What this means is that women are emotionally wired to think about how they feel in a way that men aren't. Because men are not wired this way, they don't tend to be as bothered by their emotions. Both husbands and wives need to have a frame of reference of what is a healthy marriage; otherwise, the entire family system suffers.

Relocating to Meet My Husband

My husband finally decided to move out from Washington and relocated to another state. Soon after he arrived, I received an unexpected phone call requesting for me and the children to join him; so we did. My mind was plagued with so many uncertainties before leaving for the fact that he had already abandoned the family for the past three years and the fear of not knowing what to expect. The fact is, he knew he left us with no financial support, neither kept in touch. I had so many unanswered questions as to how life would be for us; will the children be able to adopt or assimilate into this new culture; most of all, how will my relationship be with my husband, knowing that I was very resentful of him. I needed to accept and trust God's forgiveness to release me from past guilt in order to move forward. It was devastating because it seemed as though I was never going to have peace in my life. Once I forgave him, I was able to make that move. However, November 1984, we finally relocated, but life was never the same. I often questioned God and asked what I have done to deserve such sufferings and painful events. There were times I felt as though my entire world collapsed, but in spite of my pains and struggles, I never doubted God, for he said his grace was sufficient to keep me.

After experiencing three years of torment, I simply couldn't see how I could get past the conflicts and challenges. There were so many painful events in my life physically, financially, and emotionally. I didn't think I could ever possibly move forward. It was not of my own will relocating to the states. God allowed me to take control of my thoughts in making that decision.

We finally relocated mid-November. It was very cold and dark as I recall, even having a snowstorm the next day which was our first experience.

The children and I had no previous experience of the weather and did not anticipate the anxiety we suffered upon our arrival. As time went by, we experienced more inclement weather; it was bitter cold, and we're not prepared to deal with the changes. What made it even worst is that my husband never made any preparations in advance. The apartment was cold and dark, and we did not have the appropriate clothing needed. We actually went through a culture shock. Not only did we go through a culture shock, but life circumstances seemed worst. It seemed like history had repeated itself even after putting the past behind me. My estrange husband, who was already assimilated into this new culture, was not the same husband and father; he lived a totally different lifestyle from what we were accustomed to. My children and I went through a great deal of stress, facing months of various unethical dilemmas. There were stressors that crippled my life and overwhelmed me; therefore, I decided to leave my husband and walk away from the marriage. It seemed as though I was just repeating the past over and over and that there would never be a moment of true happiness.

Here I am now, residing in another state with seven children, having no family support, no money, and unemployed. There wasn't any stability or mobility in my family life. I felt powerless; my life was surrounded by more conflicts and disappointments than I could ever dream of. Three months after relocating, I got pregnant with my eighth child. By then, I was forced to make a choice, to leave my husband and marriage. Unfortunately, I took the courage and finally walked out from the marriage with my seven children. My only plea was that I wanted to return back to the Virgin Islands where I felt secure, but it was impossible since I had already sold all my furniture and spent all of my savings to buy our airfare; by then, I was financially broke. I was tired and being tired of all the disappointments, the crises, pains, and challenges and refused to live in this condition anymore.

I wanted to create a safe environment for my children. I wanted a new life. I wanted to start my life all over and felt it was my obligation as a single parent to value what was in my children's best interest.

Could you imagine what it was like having to go through such experiences within this new culture where you knew no one? However, I felt like a prisoner in my own mind and body.

However, I was determined to walk out of the abusive relationship, so I finally took the courage one morning, formed a circle with my children, prayed and asked God for his guidance. After the prayer, I took my children, left the apartment, and walked out, even though I had no idea where we would be sleeping that night. All I knew was that I was determined to leave the relationship, never to return. I had been abused and neglected too many times and was tired of being tired of the same vicious cycle, dealing with an estrange husband who had not only became a stranger but also an alcoholic. The saddest thing is that my husband never admitted of having a problem nor was he ever a believer of the word. I took the initiative to act in faith, believing that no matter what happened, I would prosper. I took my children and left, believing a change could only be proposed and be effective if it was forced. I anticipated that change by leaving my husband and searching for answers. I wanted to overcome the painful moments of my life regardless of the consequences.

Despite my troubles, I continued to seek the Lord, applied faith in making all of my decisions. I experienced some uncertainties as I tried to identify my reason for leaving my husband. I had doubts and fears that crippled me because of the complexity of the situation I was facing at the moment. I was determined to start a new life for me and my children, looking forward for a brighter tomorrow.

Many times leaving an abuse relationship is not only emotionally difficult but can also be life threatening. Statistics shows women are seventy times more likely to be killed after leaving their abusive partner. Women also believe it's their fault and that they can change their assailants, not realizing the changes involved. We need to use wisdom taking the appropriate action to end the abuse. Talk to God; deepen your relationship with him by prayer, for prayer is one of the first place to begin. Ask him for help and direction. Talk to him like you would talk to a friend.

As we talk to God by faith, believing his promises, we then are able to forgive the people who have done us wrong and let go of the past. Harboring feelings of anger and resentments only causes more pain and punishments upon or psychological being.

Hope and Victory throughout Life Crisis

In separating myself from my husband, I felt helpless and hopeless. During the early stages, I looked upon myself as a failure, having neither families nor sense of a community. However, I felt overwhelmed! Knowing that some of my expectations perhaps were unreasonably high! Disillusionment was enormous! Anticipated improvements may have also been ridiculous! It created many frustrations.

Upon departing from the cold, dark apartment, I stood by the roadside with my seven children while I was also five months pregnant. That morning, a car stopped, and the driver asked if everything was okay with me. My response was, "Yes," but deep within my heart, I knew our lives were in danger and at risk because I had no intentions of going back to the apartment. I did not feel comfortable talking about my situation to a stranger who I never met. Later that same day, about mid-afternoon, the same woman drove by again and asked, "Is everything alright?" I nodded my head and my tears began to drop. She finally realized everything was not all right. I believe the woman was convinced in her own mind that everything was not all right like I said. She then identified herself, stating that she was a social worker from DCF (Department of Children and Family Services). She said that someone had called to report that there was a pregnant woman standing on the corner of the street for a few hours with seven children. The social worker informed me that the children would be taken into custody and would be placed in foster homes until I got situated. I had no alternative but to comply as she assured me that my children would be fine and would be united with me as soon as I got situated. The family structure was interrupted. What seemed to be normal had now become more of an illusion. Both the children and I were very much confused for fear of not knowing how to deal with the situation as well as our own feelings. The DCF worker was very helpful and handed me a list of phone numbers in order to seek adequate resources.

That same day, my children were taken from me and were placed in foster homes. I had no idea where I would be laying my head that night, but a stranger invited me into her house. I was truly gracious even though I was a bit hesitant to accept her offer. I was five months pregnant and felt so helpless. The sense of helplessness gave me the strength to accept life including its situations as well as created feelings of acceptance, delivering my helplessness to God, allowing him to take control of the ultimate circumstances. A I allowed God to rectify the situation in removing all obstacles, I continued to trust him for guidance *in taking* whatever actions possible to correct the situation as *long as they were not harmful.* I looked toward a healing process including redemption and hope to whatever may have seemed hopeless. In maintaining this attitude, I was able to redeem my helplessness and took an active spiritual stance. This stance leaves ultimate justice and retribution in God's hands while we do what we can. *However, God justifies any and all of our circumstances* spiritually; it is essential to walk in harmony with God by faith. We will experience many trails in life that may discourage and defeat us, but we must always remain steadfast in Christ, while facing the oppositions and discouragements, knowing that we can and will be delivered. Just remember our timing is different from God's timing. So please learn to exercise faith.

The DCF social worker took me to the foster homes every weekend to visit my children. It might not have been the best situation because my children still talk about the bad experiences they had while placed into the foster home. The social worker acted as a central coordinating point in my life at the moment. Although it was heartbreaking to leave my children, she reassured me that my children would be well taken care of and that as soon as I got situated, they would be reunited them with me. The social worker instructed me to focus on my pregnancy and seek affordable housing so that my children could be reunited with me before the birth of my eighth child.

Finally, as time drew near for my eighth child to be born, my life became even more challenging. The very first time I went to the health center to receive prenatal care, I was advised to terminate the pregnancy. They felt that because I already had seven children and was dealing with so many other crises in my life, it was not in my best interest to keep the baby. I was devastated. So after that first visit, I never returned for prenatal care. As it was time to go into labor, that day was a stormy day; the wind blew so hard that the streets were covered with leaves and branches. As I continued to walk to the hospital to give birth, my contractions got worst. All I could do was pray and ask God for help in this situation. Every time my contractions got worst, I stopped, took a deep breath, and called upon the Lord. It so happened that one of the times I was having contractions, I stopped, and a huge tree collapsed right behind me. The Lord protected me from further danger. I finally arrived at the hospital and gave birth to a healthy baby boy who is now an educator/acting school principal. I thank God for his love, power, and his divine protection and how he helped me kept my sanity in making this transition, allowing me to give birth to this wonderful young man. He is such a blessing.

My children were finally reunited with me after I was discharged from the hospital. They were very happy to be with their mom and their baby brother. Most individuals who lived below poverty level with low socioeconomic status and low-level education is faced with various barriers. Extreme poverty presents a challenge, but we can make every effort to overcome such challenges into empowering our circumstances.

A year after my eighth child was born, I tried to reconcile with my husband, but the marriage was irreparable because of his alcoholism. My life was a total disaster. He was unemployed while I worked two jobs. Unfortunately, it was very difficult coming home and having to face many unexpected crisis and fear of the unknown. I had many sleepless nights, yet, had to be at work the next day.

However, I decided to seek help from the Lord by praying and fasting for two days. By the third day, my prayers were answered.

Believe it or not, after I returned home from work, my daughter said, "Mommy, Daddy said he went to visit his brother and would be back later." Well, that later never arrived because he never came back. Again, the Lord heard my supplication and was touched with the infirmities of my heart... Many storms crippled my life, including my spiritual walk with God. Upon relocating to the states, the faith denomination I am affiliated too did not exist, therefore my children and I worshiped at home every Sabbath. As the lord impressed on my heart to minister to others, I began ministering where I came in contact with many families and individuals who also belonged to the same denomination but didn't have a place of worship. As the membership grew, we rented a place of worship and later purchased a building with the help of head quarters. The church administration was heavily laid upon me for years before a pastor was appointed. Head quarters later appointed three men to assist with the church administration since the church culture does not promote women as pastors. As time went by, I suffered a great deal of persecution. These men became my greatest opponent leading to one of the worst storms of my life. As the lord permits, this chapter of my life will truly be revealed.

For victory belongs to us, once we declare the power of the living God, he will always come through, for there is no failure in God. Remember, he promised to deliver us from all of our afflictions. Claim God's promises into your life, for there is no problem that he cannot heal, but we must fix our eyes, minds and heart on him in the process.

Struggles of Prejudices/ Discrimination

Seeking adequate housing was a challenge. I was faced with numerous humiliations, oppositions, and discrimination by various landlords. Once I told the landlords I had seven children, they told me the apartment had been taken, or it's no longer for rent while it was still vacant. Other landlords told me, "I am sorry, but you have too many children." I had someone called about the same apartment and was told she could have it because she said she had no children. After discussing the situation with the social worker, she advised me not to disclose any information about my children unless asked. She also told me that I should tell the landlords I have fewer children since it was unusual for many households to have that many children. Single parents who have large families tend to be more discriminated against, especially African Americans, when it comes to seeking adequate housing.

According to recent studies, out of 50 percent of the median income, 30 percent of the income goes toward rent. There is a severe need for affordable housing and that economics shifts have profoundly impacted the condition of housing for many. A major problem I found during my research while completing my social work degree is that the inner cities have a disproportionate share of persons who have difficulty paying standard market rates for housing and a lack of employment. Another valuable contemporary lesson I learned while going through my own experiences is that people who migrate to this country with a different accent are often ridiculed or discriminated against.

As a society, it is time that people realize that we are all equal in God's eyes. The fact that a person may be in a better position economically does not make them better than others. As a society, we may be from different cultural backgrounds, religion, race, and ethnicity, but this doesn't make us a lesser person. We may be fortunate to be a millionaire or living a middle-class lifestyle which is a wonderful thing, but it does not make us a better person. What really matters is the life we live on earth and the relationships we share; we are all God's divine creation. The abundance of wealth we possess places us in certain classes as well as allowing us to live a comfortable life which is wonderful. For the time will come when we must all die, leaving all our possessions behind and must all appear before the judgment seat of Christ to give an account of our works, whether it be good or whether it be evil.

As individuals, we must learn to respect each other's cultures and stop judging people by the color of their skin, nationality, religious background, or culture. This society must recognize the extreme importance of other culture's language and reflect the importance in our use of terms given the change of times in which we live, realizing our own cultural values and beliefs.

I remembered when I relocated to the states to meet my husband, people addressed my children as Jamaicans when, indeed, they are U.S. born citizens. Most people are not aware that the USVI is part of the United States. Many times, people use nontraditional terms such as blacks, white, Hispanic, Indian, or African American which may not seem appropriate where in other cases where newly emerging terms seem appropriate. As a society, we must learn to be sensitive to each other's cultures and avoid all prejudices. It is my assumption that in order for a single parent to survive, communities must provide an adequate level of functioning within systems that will allow them to achieve at least a minimal acceptable quality of life. We need an economic base that will produce jobs, relevant education, and the freedom to pursue at least an education base on our interests without fear and being stereotyped.

My children had difficulty assimilating themselves within the school system. They often complained about the treatment they received from their peers. We were humiliated and oppressed. Could you imagine what it was like for a single mother of eight coming to a new culture, having no social networks, family, and friends and having to face such humiliation and oppression People need social networks, supportive environment, and other forms of resources to strengthen human relatedness, recognition, and affirmation especially in the times of crisis. I often questioned the quality of services received from many institutions, especially the advice given to me at the time of my pregnancy which left me very troublesome.

My son is the most loving and caring son any mother can wish for. It's indeed another great miracle performed in my life, knowing we walk by faith and not by sight. God has been truly good to me. He has been my focus and my strength, knowing that he promised throughout the Book of Joshua "to be strong and to be of good courage, neither be afraid, neither is dismayed, for the lord thy god is with thee whether so ever thou goest." We must believe that God will never and will never fail us.

Despite all my challenges, God has given me victory for ashes. Unless we learn to develop a personal relationship with God, we may never know about his great power and love. A person can attend all the church services of his/her life, never miss a service, and still never know about the power of God or know who God is. People can know the right thing to do, have the right answer, and still choose wrong.

Hope and Victory
through Life Crises

The various crises of my life have been my driving force to self-determination and self-sufficiency. My goal was to become self-sufficient, be a positive role model to my children, and to pursue economic stability. The journey may have been very challenging but was determined to empower myself into breaking the cycle of poverty and to be an over-comer. Essentially, individuals can feel helpless especially not being able to take control over their own lives while going through the storm. Feelings of powerlessness may produce an existential sense of anxiety which may cause depression. I was determined to escape depression; therefore, I engaged in all the activities I could while my children attended school.

Despite my challenges, I remained focused and committed and faithful to God. I focused on taking care of the needs of my children rather than their wants. I made a concrete decision never to get involved in another relationship since my main focus and belief was centered upon self-determination and self-sufficiency. Despite all my failures, disappointment, and challenges, I will always continue to have a special love in my heart like I have never been hurt. I was very dedicated in establishing an independent base of power within the family structure as I played both roles to my eight children, having four boys and four girls.

In gaining my own economic independence, my mission was to create a family model which would establish a basis for commitment, obligation, social support, and family values. It is my belief that families must build and establish communities that are excited and meaningful in a loving, caring environment in every stage of life, our family relationships presents both joy and challenges. Learning to understand our own emotions, behaviors and communication style can help strengthen family relationships effectively.

Our values tend to help us make demands that are efficient and effective. Every single parent/head of household must obtain the perseverance to obtain the skills, education, and resources needed to break the cycle of poverty as well as identify their own strengths and weaknesses. Families must learn to pray together; for the family that prays together, stays together. I believe in family togetherness and strong moral values. As a child, I was taught to have strong moral values which I was able to pass down to my own children which has helped them to become the persons they are. We must be interconnected as a family, given that we must be able to create a sense of social order, family ties, and thereby, must take the responsibility to care for each other.

Every single-headed household must work to transform social and economic realities and open systems that will support family values. By creating an open system model, I was able to have considerable influence on the family model as well as my family dynamics. Our environment must be recognized as a critical point in every family member. Identification of survival is the primary reason for existence of all family members. The open system model emphasizes on family dependency as the product of interactions within each environment. As a single parent, I assisted and supported my children in every way possible into building a family structure with good moral values. I stressed the value of education to my children as my aunt had passed down to me so that as they become young adults, they too will be able to take a positive approach in their academic endeavor.

Life Transformation/ Purpose/Destination

After graduating from college with my associate degree was the most joyful moment for me and my children. I could never forget the excitement they all demonstrated. This was really the turning point for all of us, believing that if Mom did, then we all can.

For instance, my second child was in high school and had already determined college was not suitable for her. After accomplishing my associate degree, she realized this was not as bad as she thought. Her exact words were, "If Mummy did it, I can do it too." She did not hesitate but attended college and obtained a BS degree in sociology and criminology.

The eldest obtained a BS in foreign languages, third child obtained master's degree in education, fourth child BS psychology, fifth child BS education, sixth child AS degree in computer science, seventh child BS nursing degree, and my eighth child obtained two master's degree, one in business administration and in ED, who is now the acting school principal. Can you believe the same child which I was advised to abort now has become the assistant school principal with two master's degree? I was practically homeless and already had seven children. I am so grateful for listening to that still small voice within me. Otherwise, my second and last child would not have been born, and perhaps, I may have lived with regrets. Thank God for his words of comfort, "For he encourage us to be strong, be not afraid, neither be dismayed for he will always be with us whither so ever thou goest."

Our God is truly a god of restoration, whatever he promised he will do.

For our God is a God of love, hope, joy, and peace. He promised to heal our wounds. God is able to give us good health, strength, freedom from all our financial provisions, hope to our hurting friends and families, help overcome depression, anxiety, fear, as well as helping us recover from bad situations.

Family Values

The values taught to me by my aunt truly paid off. Despite my failures and challenges, I turned out to be an educated, professional woman who worked within a diverse and disadvantaged population. My aunt was the motivating factor who influenced me to internalize those values in creating a self-image and a level of dignity in self-determination. She always expressed that formal education is truly the key to success. As a single household parent, there were times I felt overwhelmed and frustrated by the abundance of responsibilities and obstacles; nevertheless, my will and determination helped me to endure. The fundamentals of family practice are essential to every household as it allows us to transform to realization of empowerment.

As I strive toward economic independence and mobility, I worked on my own personal guilt of rejection, abuse, and neglect while I kept them away from my children. For example, I would be the strongest person in their presence; yet, shed my tears while they were sleeping.

My willingness to keep my own personal feelings away from my children was a driving force to create a new identity so that they, themselves, will pattern after. I committed to a higher standard of personal conduct as I handled each situation carefully, not neglecting my children by any means. I tried to be the best parent possible in doing my best.

The reality of it all is that as a family, we prayed together, which helped establish a sense of stability and order within the family structure. My family was strengthened physically, spiritually, financially, and emotionally, even though I was not financially independent. The main purpose of our family system was to respect and love each other.

Every one of us played an important role in nurturing each other. As a family we have the responsibility of creating a safe, supportive environment raising our children in the fear of the Lord. Some family members may never adhere to the principals and instructions, but we must always love them unconditionally and pray for them.

Overcoming Discrimination

During the time of my crisis, I learned some valuable lessons which helped create my own identity. A month after moving into my first apartment before my eighth child was born, I developed a strategic plan in addressing my own shortcomings in putting my priorities in order. The fact was that the apartment was not in good living conditions. I decided to seek for a better apartment. It was not an easy task because most landlords discriminated against me, refusing to rent to me because they felt I had too many children. Finally, I met a landlord who was willing to visit the place where I lived. The landlord immediately evaluated my family situation as he visited my old apartment. He was moved with compassion and had me sign a lease so that I could move to a new apartment immediately. That apartment was already reserved for someone else but gave it to me after seeing my condition. Even though we needed a four-bedroom based on state regulations, the landlord allowed us to move into a three-bedroom for the sake of the newborn baby. It was a struggle, but through much prayers and perseverance, God heard my supplications. Life was indeed a challenge, but I never doubted God for one moment. God again came through with another miracle. I was very much impacted by having suffered much prejudices and discrimination. I made a decision to develop my own goals and objectives, establish my short-term goal as well as a long-term goal. The key to this approach definitely benefited both me and my children. I realized the proportion of black single-headed households as well as single mothers were overlooking in the world of employment, housing, and other related services. It is important for families, especially single-headed households, to become aware of the importance of education as it will avoid them to be employed in low paying jobs and to become economically independent. There are also racial disparities which is overlooked. For example, racial disparities in wealth holdings have been greater than income differences since the 1960. The question remains, "Shall we ever overcome such disparities?"

Single-headed household, especially females, tend to have a high incidence of poverty. The major reason is that the demands of childcare often make the mother unavailable to work. They often become dependent of public transportation and public assistance which puts them below poverty level. As single-headed households, we need to make every effort in taking advantage of the training programs made available which will allow at least a decent form of education to adequately find employment for self-sufficiency. For those not in the labor force or unemployed, poverty seems to be very high, giving them a lesser quality of life. There might be a number of reasons for being unemployed such as lack of childcare, unskilled, uneducated, or lack of the necessary skills to meet a job requirement. We must educate ourselves academically if we want to escape poverty.

Racial and gender discrimination are also other factors preventing a person from obtaining employment. While families living in poverty are the working poor, they are also uneducated which results in low-paying jobs. They have limited skills and limited education. My life circumstances were not easy, every day was a challenge. I worked full-time as well as part-time for minimum wage. My wages did not allow enough income for my family's basic needs. Yes, I have been there and can identify and relate to such deficiencies and inequalities.

There will always be inequalities between race and class especially in terms of single-headed household. Based on my own observation, single-headed households especially women are more likely:

- To be poor
- Die in childbirth
- Separate from their spouse
- Live in single-family household
- Lacked or have limited education
- Have their children place in foster homes

- Faced child abuse
- Babies are born to teenage-wed mothers
- Live in subsidized housing
- Their sons suffer corporal punishment.

In fact, some people may feel most African Americans face little or no discrimination in jobs, housing, or education and that many of the difficulties they face is a result of lack of motivation. Based on my own experience, single-female-headed households are not treated equally in terms of housing, education, and employment which is mainly due to discrimination. This is why I believe we should capture the aspirations for self-determination and self-empowerment despite the inequalities that surround us. Once we are able to gain an education, enter the workforce. We will find that it is possible to become independent of others. By obtaining a good education, one can definitely create a new identity for themselves. Remember, with God all things are possible.

Areas around which such prejudices and oppression often occur are gender, race, ethnicity, sexual orientation, age, and disability. Prejudices are intimately tied to values and may affect how a person feels while discrimination is acting out those prejudices. These actions are clearly observed among individual differences especially in the labor force. Access to employment in some instances may limit opportunities for single-headed households due to homemaker roles, day care, and transportation because work opportunities are not readily available close to home. Lack of transportation may limit access to employment. Inadequate childcare may also limit one's ability to be engaged in some type of employment as well as other pursuits in which they may have an interest. Every individual essentially controls his or her own destination to an extent, but god has the ability to control the outcome of all our circumstance.

My philosophy is that through hard work and persistence and self-determination, a person can overcome any barriers or limitations. My personal life situation is considered to be a systematic evidence.

Self-Empowerment

Acknowledging my own limitations gave me the power to take control of my own future. I first enrolled in a secretarial training program after my eighth child was born. It was very difficult at the beginning, but I persevered. Just before graduating, the instructor made an announcement about a data entry position available through the state and that everyone should apply. I doubted myself and refused to apply for the position because I felt many of the other students were more qualified. My instructor noticed that I did not submit an application; therefore, he requested that I fill one out because he felt I was the most qualified candidate and had the drive and potential to succeed.

Sometimes, we are too critical on ourselves, especially after losing focus. At the time, my mind was plagued with lots of what ifs. Why would a mother of eight who has no formal education, no transportation be qualified? Few weeks after submitting the job application, I received the results by mail stating that I was selected for the job. Too many times, single mothers lack self-confidence, which defeat their purpose in life. We need to be motivated, avoid doubt as we persevere to overcome barriers in accomplishing our goals. Our circumstances may not allow us to live up to the Jones's, but we can sure live up to our expectations, never underestimate or doubt our potential of what we can and cannot do. Everyone has skills and abilities that have not been recognized. Just remember, we all have choices in life it is all about a matter of perspective. Some of us may have been burned in the past by making bad choices and are afraid to take risk. The bottom line is we all need to learn how to make good choices and wise decisions throughout our development stage and not be afraid. Always avoid making the same mistakes over.

A year after employment, I started college. My challenges became even greater but was determined to succeed and to create a better quality of life for me and my children. One may ask, "How did you survive or overcame such obstacles?" May I say through faith, self-determination, and perseverance. My goal was to pursue higher education in order to make a difference in the lives of people. I wanted to give back to society, especially single-headed households, seeing that I can identify to them. I realize many times single parents can feel pressured and discouraged which causes them to defeat their goals and purposes.

I am a strong advocate of higher education as well as self-sufficiency. I hope every single parent realize they have more potential than they could ever dream of, apply their transferable skills, have the ability to take control of their lives, and accept all the free training programs which may be available to them. Believe it or not, these free training programs are indeed a stepping stone academically to personal success. Without these training programs, perhaps I would not have accomplished my goals.

Employment and Self-Determination

After obtaining my associate degree in psychology and a minor in sociology, I took a break so that I could spend quality time with my children due to the fact that I was employed full-time and part-time as well. It was a struggle, but through self-determination, I accomplished my short-term goal as well as my long-term goal. Every single parent who is facing homelessness and poverty can find the road to self-sufficiency, but you must take action.

My long-term goal was to become a social worker in order to assist many people. The social worker that was with me during my crisis became the central point of my life. She played a significant role, allowing me to develop a strong desire to become a social worker so that I can give back to society. A good social worker directs, give the necessary resources, and help mobilize families. Perhaps without the guidance and support of the social worker, it could not have been made possible for me to escape the difficulties of life. Individuals who are at a disadvantage need to take full charge for their own failures and set realistic goals that will allow them to become self-sufficient and feel empowered. It is rewarding and gratifying to have provided In Home Based reunification Services to families and individuals following the removal of a child(ren) due to abuse or neglect.

When I started my career, I worked as a data entry operator. I earned $15,000 a year which could barely cover my expenses, so I also worked a part-time job. The fact is men earn more than women for the same job performed. Statistics shows that women have fewer work experience and attain less education than men of the same age. The reason is that while men usually work continuously from the end of schooling the labor force, woman has historically been interrupted during childbearing and child-rearing years. The earning gap between females and males has historically been quite large in the United States. Based on recent studies, females have typically earned about 60 percent that of males. However, through our employment, my salary was always the lowest since I had the lowest position.

I continued to work and attended college so that I could attain my bachelor's degree in psychology. It seemed as though I would have never earned that degree. It took me eight years to complete my bachelor's degree and two additional years to complete my LMSW social work degree. It has been most rewarding. It marks the beginning of a significant and exciting transition throughout my career. Whether a person is out of school or returning to school, new doors of opportunities can be opened. We just need the ability to gain new ways of thinking into creating a better way of life. My entire lifestyle has been devoted to my children, work, and higher education most importantly to God. I never missed a parent's conference. Children need to know that they are supported and loved, and therefore, I was very much involved in their school activities. I remembered the day I surprised my son at his football game. He told me sitting in the audience he was so happy when he saw me in the crowd that he played three times harder. He scored higher than the other team members allowing his team to be victorious. As parents we must set aside quality time to be part of our children's curriculum which could be highly beneficial.

I was also a very protective parent. We didn't have much, but we had each other. It certainly felt promising and exciting to know that I found new ways to accomplish my hopes and dreams for the future. One must have the right attitude in order to achieve academic success.

Even though the potential of the future may seem untold, we should never doubt ourselves with our ability to achieve success because the feeling of guilt can defeat our high spirits of motivation. Please be aware of these feelings and recognize that these signs are only a form of growth in allowing you to take preventive measures so that your dreams can become a reality.

Perhaps what I found out to be most controversial during my career is that most unmarried mothers remain unmarried, remain on welfare roles, and have babies. However, there seems to be a steady growth in the percentage of female-headed households as well as deterioration within the family systems and family values. Despite the increase of female-headed household, studies show that higher welfare benefits increase the probability of female headship and lower the probability of marriage. I also found out that daughters coming from welfare families are more likely to receive welfare themselves at a later age than those of non-welfare parents.

Single-headed household, especially females, must empower themselves by obtaining higher education in order to break the cycle of poverty. Don't let anyone tell you otherwise. All the excuses in the world will not give you self-satisfaction. I was determined not to become another statistic, and therefore, I became very proactive in defining my goals and objectives.

Because my life had been consumed by so much painful crises: abuse, divorce, discrimination, oppression, etc., I did not want to be stigmatized as the lady on welfare with eight children. Society tends to view and stigmatize families on welfare, not realizing that each family situation is different. I came from a family background that valued strong work ethics and was mission-driven to accomplish my long-term goal.

Just remember that a quitter never wins. My only consolation was that with Christ, all things are possible. I never forgot the verse of scripture that says, "I can do all things through Christ which strengthens me." Today, I am a very proud mother, knowing that all of my eight children are college graduates and that most of them are employed in their professional careers. I am pleased to know that I was a positive role model in allowing them to be also goal-oriented. The spirit of God continues to empower me as I am now living the best years of my life. To God be the glory for the great things he has done. For I am truly blessed and highly favored.

Remember those who put their trust in God, will never be defeated nor put to shame, for he promised to be our defense.

Moving Forward

It was not a smooth journey, but by the grace of God, the family preserved. We embraced the tough times and the unchangeable, believing for the changeable. There is nothing too hard for God. We all can overcome the crises of our lives as long as we put our trust in God. All the disadvantages and stumbling blocks can be overcome. The truth is whether a person has gone through financial loss, joblessness, inadequate housing, lack of transportation, inadequate childcare, mentally and physically challenged, that person can make a difference through faith self-perseverance and self-determination.

My daughter who attended school of nursing always had a passion to help others and to become a nurse and work as a nurse. During her last year in college, her entire world collapsed while living on campus. She is the sweetest and most loving child. Intellectually, she always maintained a GPA of 3.0, very committed to her academics. While attending college, she was faced with humiliation and manipulation, especially in her clinical rotation; her religious beliefs were questioned. As a concerned parent, I also had to deal with the situation. I would hate to believe that my daughter was being targeted based on the fact that she constantly had difficulty accessing her assignment from the computer, always needed to have her password changed, as well as having continuous technical problems. Despite of the growing pains she faced, I continued to voice my concerns to the school administration. My daughter was left feeling ostracized for voicing her concerns and, later, developed psychological problems. One day while at work, I received one of the worst phone call a mother would expect. I received a phone call from the school stating that my daughter needed to be evaluated by a psychiatrist and should not return to school until released. However, as my daughter's situation worsened, she was admitted to the psychiatric unit, followed by several other hospitalizations. This impacted the entire family. When serious illness or disability strikes a family member, the family as a whole is affected by the disease process and by the entire health care experience. It has not been easy for our family dealing with this situation. Her life has never been the same. It was heart-wrenching to see my child suffer such condition. A child who had such high expectation of accomplishing her goals in becoming a nurse, now, has to deal with the challenges of the unknown. We may never know what happened during the four years she lived on campus. I hope that one day everything will be revealed. She finally earned her nursing degree, but life has never been the same. In spite of all my challenges, I never doubted myself but trusted God for deliverance. My daughter has made great improvements by God's grace. She has a three-year son which I do have legal custody off. Knowing my steps are ordered by God. I do believe the lord has a plan for his life.

Remember, I was exactly where most disadvantaged single-headed household is today, but I never felt sorry for myself. I was too busy trying to find means and ways to become economically independent. Disappointments and rejection will come, but always remember, you must never give up on your aspirations and dreams. We must come to realization and get out of our comfort zone to make things happen.

There are several job programs targeted directly to single-headed households that provide individuals the tools and resources needed to eventually find suitable employment and become self-sufficient. It also allows them to increase their capital which could lead to long-term improvement in both their employability and their lifetime earnings. Most individuals do not take advantage of this opportunity to adequately become economically independent.

Affordable housing can also add stability to the lives of single-headed households. It can help their children improve academically and increase their chances for gainful employment. Women's ability to achieve economic security through employment is critically linked to today's economic success. While education seem to be the key to women's equality, postsecondary education for low-income families has decreased because of high cost of tuition. It so happened that while enrolled in post education, I maintained a GPA of 3.5, which allowed me to obtain free scholarships in pursuing my LMSW degree. This is truly indeed another great miracle, trusting God for victory.

Exercising Faith /Gaining Success

I truly believe our steps are ordered by God. We must believe in his promises, for it has been pronounced that we shall be the head and not the tail, we shall be the lender and not the borrower. While we are faced with many trials and life challenges, we must believe that God sees and knows it all. As we apply faith and allow Gods holy spirit to take control of our lives, we can can be an over comer and to enjoy all of Gods blessings and promises. Our goal is to be believe and to be receptive in allowing his blessings to be fulfill into our lives. We must completely surrender and allow God to transform our minds by faith so that we can find peace, true happiness, and success. By cleansing our mind, body and soul from all spiritual con-tamination we can have power over darkness. The same promise that was made to Abraham can take effect into our lives through faith. for "faith is the substance of things hope for, the evidence of things not seen.". At the time of my struggles and my life circumstances, I, trusted God and asked him, daily to help me walk in true faithfulness and holiness so that I could be bless with the blessing of Abraham. The lord granted me that favor. To God be the glory.

I believe Success and victory can only be achieved by obtaining all of Gods promises, only if we continue to walk in faith, obedience and true righteousness. Self gratification allows us to enjoy the works of our labor and to be successful, but the greatest success is eternal life. According to the book Joshua "this book of the law shall not depart out thy mouth , but thou shall meditate therein day and night that thou may observe to do according to all that is written therein, for thou shall make thy way prosperous and then thou shall have good success. Remember there is no failure in God and that is prom-ises are sure.

Work Environment

At the time of employment, working for the same organization for twenty nine years, I attended college until I earned my LMSW degree. My goal was to bridge the gap into other target job opportunities for career advancements. However, having obtained my LMSW degree, it made life even more challenging. The fact is, even though I was employed with the same agency for twenty-nine years that promoted growth and upward mobility, I was discriminated against almost every promotion that fitted into my academic success and qualifications.

Imagine, I was still working as office assistant even though I had already obtained a master's degree in social work. We work in a bureaucratic system where people are filled with preconceived ideas that truly discriminate women of color, especially those with an accent. Personal/social relationships within the workplace are another phenomenon that disadvantage women and minority employees. However, most times, I was excluded from important networks. Economic discrimination in some cases show that women of color are not virtually favored in terms of promotion. Agencies rigidly define their purpose and services. Most employees remain very formal, following policies and procedures, and supervisors tend to discourage innovation and flexibility among staff because they are very formal in their decision-making. It is very important to understand the legal basis on which supervisors operate. The African director fought some battles during the time of my employment. The fact is she was very assertive, non-judgmental, and very honest in her practices which created some ethical dilemmas. She was the type of supervisor who encouraged and promoted self-improvement. She was really my driving force as she encouraged me to obtain several certifications. For example, she requested that I completed the following certification programs including Resume Writer, Global Career Facilitator, Myers-Briggs Assessor, APT which gave me access to dominated prestigious occupations.

I had been employed for fifteen years before she became the director and supervisor. During this fifteen-year-period, I suffered a great deal of racism, oppression, and discrimination in terms of job promotions. There was a time I submitted a job questionnaire to human resources to be reviewed for promotion because I was working out of my job classification and needed to be promoted. The promotion was denied; therefore, I filed a grievance through my union rights. After having attended several hearings and arbitration, I was victorious. My supervisor was told that I was definitely working out of class and needed to be promoted; otherwise, those job duties would have to be taken away since they are not part of my job classification. Well the moral of the story is the same week I returned to work, I was left with almost nothing to do because most of my job assignments were taken away from me, whether they were in or out of my job classification. I was deprived from performing any job duties and sat at my desk for three long years; day in, day out with hardly any work assignment. I was treated so unfairly during my years of labor. One of my job assignments was to open all the incoming mail and distribute them to the appropriate personnel. Unfortunately, there were two occasions I found letters that was written from other superiors within the agency to the new assigned directors stating that I should never be promoted as this was their goal. I was devastated and cried for days. The only person who knew about the letters was a supervisor from another unit on the second floor who always encouraged me since he knew the unethical dilemmas that existed within the office. He said to me that my education has become a threat to many since I was the only person in the office with a master's degree. I destroyed the letters and never disclosed the information to anyone for fear of repercussions.

I worked so hard in and out of my job classification, applied for every job promotion I was qualified for. I would get the interview but was never considered for the job promotion. The fact is, the very same people who got the promotions would shadow me at times.

During my twenty-six year of employment, the director approached me and said that he received a complaint from a client stating that I had given him information unrelated to the agency's website which I was fully aware of. At the end of the day, he informed me that human resources requested that I should wait until I received a call before returning to work. A week later, I received a letter stating that I was placed on administrative paid leave for sixty days until an investigation was completed. I was also prohibited from entering the office building to get my personal belongings. Three months later, I received a letter from human resources stating based on the conduct of their investigation, I have been terminated. Employers have no loyalty to their employees. I gave more than a hundred percent while I performed my job duties. They treated me like I was a total stranger. After twenty-six years of service, you thought there would be some empathy. I never had a negative report, never late, excellent attendance, good performance evaluation, received numerous complimentary letters from clients regarding my services, and never a complaint except that incident. At the moment, I said to myself, *They finally succeeded with what they have been trying for years*, because I was constantly put down and unrecognized for my excellent performance and was overlooked with every promotion as they became available. Because of my strong faith in God, I was able to survive within that sort of environment. That still small voice within me kept on saying, *Don't give up, for the Lord will carry you through. For this mountain is bigger than you think and that only God could fight your battles.* So I went before my Lord in prayer and fasting continually. I finally consulted the union president who assisted and attended several of my hearings, litigations, and arbitrations. My only hope was to trust God for my deliverance. I personally built an alter in my bedroom, where I communicated with God on a daily basis seeking for divine interventions. Days before my last hearing I felt all alone and had no strength left, because I received no support especially from the ones I expected to. The only thing which kept me going was my daily 5:30 a.m. prayer line and God's grace. Thanks, God, for cavalry. The morning before attending my last hearing, I asked the lord to use my union president as my mouthpiece like he used Moses to lead the children of Israel, since I was so exhausted. Believe it or not, the lord answered my prayers that same day. Upon my arrival to the hearing, the union president said to me. Today I will be your mouthpiece and will do all the talking, please say nothing, I was so relieved and astonished to see that my prayers were answered that same day. What a miracle. The word of the lord says, we receive not because we ask not. I encourage every believer to trust God for answers to all of their problems. for whatever you ask in faith believing, he will grant it. The same day I returned from the hearing, I went to sleep, during that time, I dreamt that I returned to work and indeed, I received notification the following day to report to work, exactly one year after my dismissal. The lord has been Good to me, because of my faith in God, I have been able to overcome many trials and hardships. I will forever worship and adore him. During that time, I had no income, so I applied for benefits. The hearing went in my favor and collected benefits. A year later, I received confirmation stating that my job was reinstated and should report to work. I was unable to file a law suit for the fact I had already signed the agreement which stated I could not under certain conditions. I know God heard my supplications and did great things for me as a result of my prayers. The same week I returned to work, I received notice stating that my hearing decision was reversed because I intentionally did not reveal important information at the hearing, and therefore, my claim was denied and had to pay back the benefits I collected. I made a payment plan and agreed to pay back the money based on their decision. I also received a letter from the Ethics Commission division stating that I had a case pending and that an investigation is being done for violating the code of ethics. The investigation was done by the ethics advisory board that dismissed the complaint because their investigation revealed there were insufficient facts based on the allegations.

When God is for you, no one can be against you. They will try but never succeed because there is power in prayer. Prayer is the most powerful weapon. No matter how those critical forces try to destroy me and put me down, God stood by my side and gave me the victory through much prayer and supplication. For I am more than a con-quer as I depended on him to change my life and help me fight my battles. Believe it or not, I could not have overcome these battles by myself. For I was being wounded over and over again.

I found out that single women are mostly trapped in low-wage jobs that comprise the majority of seasonal and part-time workers and are paid less than men in comparable occupations. If women are paid comparable wages, then they are more likely to gain eco-nomic freedom, become social workers, nurses, computer analysts, dental assistant, computer programmers. There has been a dramatic growth in the number of jobs paying low-income. Women definitely need to improve their social conditions and gain a level of empow-erment. We are literally what we think. I actually had to change the way I think and entertain new thoughts to bring about a change. As individuals, we cannot change our thoughts without changing our lives, whether it's for the best or the worst, while going through the process. While immersing myself in the right thoughts, I was able to become exactly the person I long to be. In order to change the way we think and to deal with the obstacles in our lives, we must first take a positive approach in overcoming all the negative circumstances that surrounds us. I was endeavoring to learn more about the aspects in which I must pursue. In the pursuit of education, if computers are going to direct my life, why not learn about some computer technol-ogy, become familiar with the training, and assume responsibility for my own action.

Most female-headed house may become overwhelmed, discour-aged, confused by everyday life stressor which can make the transi-tion somewhat difficult. Once I become intrinsically aware of my skills and got involved in higher leaning, I gained the great bene-fits of becoming a positive role model to my children. Everyone can improve academically by developing strong personal confidence. My biggest barriers were fears of rejection and fears of failure. Too many times we allow anxiety and self-doubt to paralyze us from achieving our goals.

My goal in becoming a social worker, ultimately, was to deal with the issues of social justice so that the client can be benefited and also to provide the ultimate guidance and resources to others to accomplish their goals. I can now attest to the legal responsibility of social workers as they become a reliable source to inform clients about the nature of services, the probability of successful outcomes, the risks, and other alternatives as clients place their trust in us in making decisions for them. I am very subjective as I avoid all personal feelings and biases in carrying out my role effectively. I can now guide and facilitate ways to advocate the rights of others especially if they cannot do it for themselves. It is in my power as a practitioner to mobilize, guide, facilitate, and develop greater mutuality and reciprocity in the client-worker relationship. I am now aware of my professional function to exercise competent judgment in upholding my ethical standards. Effectiveness and accountability must be focused on the results and effects of a person's willingness and commitment to empowerment. Having educated myself in the social worker field allowed me to consciously view how social workers must network in providing emotional resources, strength for meeting the need of human relatedness, recognition, and affirmation. I am also a highly dedicated competent human service professional with extensive experience in determining program eligibility, counseling, career guidance, case management, and a strong background in community outreach-based programs, global career facilitator. Facilitated many workshops including: resume writing, cover letter, job search strategies, interviewing techniques, over forty, administered the Myers-Briggs assessment, career guidance, resume critique, career exploration, self-esteem and motivation, case management, and many more. According to the National Association of Social Workers Inc, if people receive adequate support and the necessary resources needed, then they can become economically independent and more likely to leave the abusive relationship.

After twenty-nine and half years, I accepted a job offer with another agency. Three months into the job, the director called me into his office and requested to have union representation. I had no clue why, so I asked why, and he said that a supervisor complained I was very disrespectful to her and the staff. An investigation was done as they questioned many of the staff and found those allegations were untrue. It seemed as though history had repeated itself. Believe it or not, I never had such an encounter with this supervisor. When I came in the morning if she was around, I would politely say, "Good morning. How are you doing," and that was it. Never saw her again during the day. I felt so hurt that after going back to my desk, I wept bitterly until I consoled myself. That same day, I immediately called human resources and requested my retirement. No question was asked except for if that was what I really wanted and my reply was most definitely. The next day, I received a phone call requesting to meet with a human resources representative at a well-known restaurant in order to fill out the retirement paperwork and to turn in my keys. I followed through the instructions, and my retirement became official.

One lesson learned is that no matter how people may try to harm you and put stumbling blocks in your way, they will never succeed. It may look as though they won the fight, but as long as God is on your side, they can never win the battle. I have so much to share but have to stop here. Hope life permits me to continue writing about my life journey. As long as God is on our side we have nothing to fear. For he is more powerful making us more than conquerors. God does not want his children to fail, but to succeed; therefore no forces of darkness can defeat us, as long as we stay under his wings, walking in true righteous and holiness.

I am now retired, enjoying spending time with my children and my nineteen grandchildren, enjoying every moment. In addition, I am so grateful to God for all my accomplishments. I worked for many years within a bureaucratic system, which strongly discriminated against me; yet God helped me, kept my integrity as well as my commitment in providing high quality service provision. I utilized my sensitivity and technical skills to all my clients. My LMSW degree gave me a depth of knowledge on social work and the systems of delivery of human services which has been utilized in different settings. I also received excellent reviews from many of the customers who attended my workshop presentations. My professionalism and service delivery were evident. I was very dedicated and committed to provide excellent services to all my customers. Here are some reviews I would like to share.

Comments from Clients

First comment:

"I have all the education {MS, MBBS, MD} training experience but is a complete novice when it comes to writing a resume. What an elegant lady, Ms. George. I have seldom met a person who could be so friendly but equally professional. She is highly motivated, knowledgeable, and skilled. Her intelligence in assessing a person's inherent capacity is a gift most people would like to have. The speed at which she could comprehend the lacuna in my resume and how it could be filled with my attributes is phenomenal. We need more personnel like Ms. George in the current position."

Second comment:

"Your job search strategy class was exceptional, and your performance was above and beyond exceptional. You provided us with a detail overview. You are a true asset to the company. I have had numerous opportunities to experience firsthand the power of having a highly educated, dedicated, and phenomenal teacher. I am proud to have you as a student and even more proud to look up to you as a mentor and, most importantly, friend."

Third comment:

"Ms. George has worked effectively with clients from all segments of the population, whether they are long-term unemployed with little education or individuals with extensive backgrounds, finding themselves unexpectedly unemployed. Customers have told us how much they appreciate Ms. George's ability to provide support, guidance, and to instill self-confidence."

Fourth comment:

Dear Ms. George,

Thank you so much presenting "Over Forty and looking for Work" at Plymouth Town Hall.

Your warmth and enthusiasm kept the attention of the group, who were from a variety of different professionals and socioeconomic backgrounds. I was impressed at the way you tailored the class to the individuals who were in attendance. I look forward to hosting similar events in the future.

My personal life experience has demonstrated extreme determination, raising eight children as a single mother as well as over-coming many crises and negative challenges in gaining self-empowerment. I hope by sharing my real-life story, someone can be benefited and help make a difference in their lives as they go through their own life challenges. My devotion and faith in God have allowed me to step out of my comfort zone, face each day as a stepping stone to reach my goals toward self-sufficiency, and provide my eight children a brighter and hopeful future. Both me and my children have pursued higher and post-education and career opportunities even though there were so many mountains to climb. Many problems, great and small presented themselves throughout my life journey as I struggled with severe heart wrenching moments. In fact learning to deal with and overcoming adversities allowed me to build resilience and character. Every crisis helped strengthened my confidence and the ability to conquer future obstacles. By building a personal relationship with god I was able to regain strength. God indeed gave me the persistence and the determination to prevail. God's holy spirit comforted me, gave me the strength and peace that passeth all understanding as I trust him by faith in overcoming the storms of my life.

About the Author

Through her hardship as a single parent of eight, Anastasie encountered many challenges, yet has proven the power of prayer and faith. Born and raised in the Caribbean West Indies, and then migrating to the United States Virgin Islands in 1971. She finally settled in United States, in 1982 where she adhered to God's calling; administering, counseling, as well as providing assistance to many individuals and families in fulfilling their life's purpose while she raised her eight children in the fear of the Lord. Now a retired LMSW social worker and community services worker, Anastasie is living a life of entrepreneurship, managing a successful business while raising her grandson as well as following the call God has on her as a writer, author and counselor.

CPSIA information can be obtained
at www.ICGtesting.com
Printed in the USA
FSHW020725250220